Maximilien Robespierre is both a hero and a villain of French history. In turbulent times, he took the country to a dark place in order to cleanse it. Read on to find out more about him.

FRENCH REVOLUTION

HE WHO STARTED THE REIGN OF TERROR
THE STORY OF MAXIMILIEN ROBESPIERRE

BIOGRAPHY BOOK FOR KIDS 9-12
CHILDREN'S BIOGRAPHY BOOKS

BABY PROFESSOR
EDUCATION KIDS

Speedy Publishing LLC

40 E. Main St. #1156

Newark, DE 19711

www.speedypublishing.com

Copyright 2017

THE ARCHITECT OF REVOLUTION

Maximilien de Robespierre was a major figure during the French Revolution, which started in 1789. He was a political theorist whose kinder and more humane qualities seem to have gotten swallowed up by his own theories.

EARLY LIFE

Robespierre was born in Arras, France in 1758. He was the oldest of four children, and the children lost their parents when Robespierre was about six years old.

MAXIMILIEN ROBESPIERRE

ARRAS, FRANCE

His mother's parents raised Robespierre and the other children. This was a kindly act, but the grandparents never stopped reminding the children of how grateful they should be, and of what a failure their father had been. As soon as he was able, Robespierre took on much of the work of caring for the other children.

Robespierre studied in Paris and earned a law degree in 1781. He returned to Arras to practice law. He had a profitable practice, but he was also known for taking on poor clients and charging them little or nothing for his work.

MAXIMILIEN ROBESPIERRE

JEAN-JACQUES ROUSSEAU

More and more, Robespierre spoke out publicly about the need for change in France. The country was heavily in debt to finance the pleasures and pastimes of the nobility and the great landowners, and there was a huge gap in possibilities and resources between the many poor and the very few rich. He was influenced by the great philosopher Jean-Jacques Rousseau and Rousseau's concept of the virtuous man who is willing to stand alone for what he knows is right.

Rousseau's public speeches, his strict code of moral values, and his work to defend the poor in court gained him the nickname "incorruptible".

LES CHARMETTES
A MUSEUM DEDICATED TO ROUSSEAU

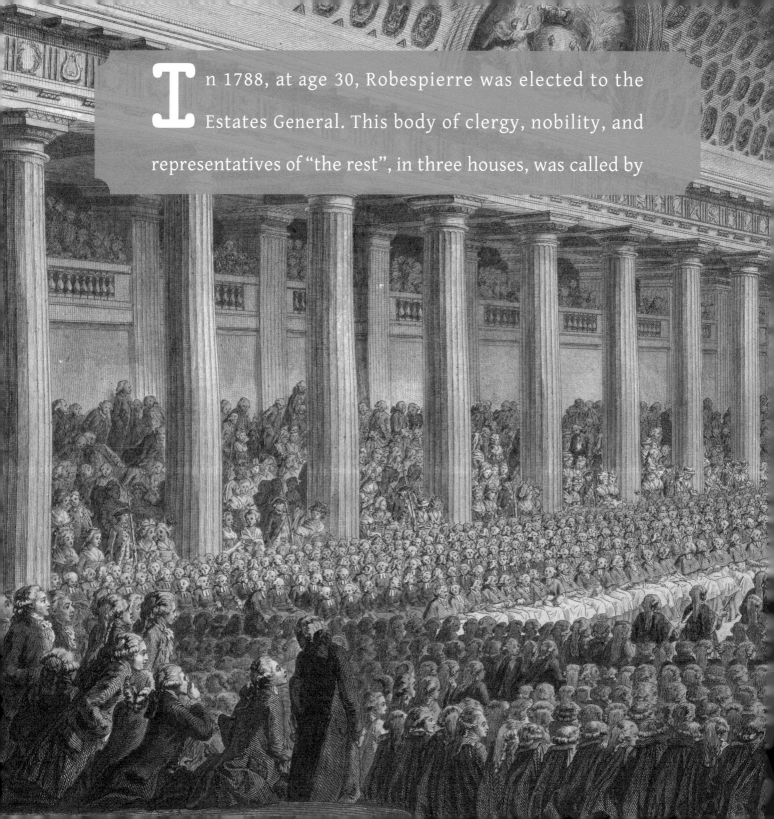

In 1788, at age 30, Robespierre was elected to the Estates General. This body of clergy, nobility, and representatives of "the rest", in three houses, was called by

the king to approve new taxes. Instead, it began a process of reforming the government, whether or not the king and the nobility wanted that.

In the assembly, Robespierre made stirring speeches attacking the king and the nobility, which made him very popular with the poor. Other members of the assembly saw him as rigid and hard to work with. It seemed that he wanted to be absolutely right rather than negotiate gradual changes and improvements. After a while, Robespierre decided he could have more effect outside of the assembly, and resigned his post.

ESTATES GENERAL

TERRACOTTA BUST OF ROBESPIERRE

TIMES OF UNREST

People may have found Robespierre difficult to work with, but his attitude closely reflected the impatience and anger of the common people. They did not want small increases in public assistance: they wanted the rich to be swept away and for the common people to share the wealth of the nation.

In early 1789, Robespierre became president of a powerful political group, the Jacobins. They represented the revolutionary thinkers who saw radical change as the only way to save France from the excesses of its rulers. Read about them in the Baby Professor book *Who Were the Jacobins?*

THE DECLARATION OF THE RIGHTS OF MAN AND CITIZENS

In 1789, Robespierre took part in writing a document that became the basis of the constitution of France, "The Declaration of the Rights of Man and Citizens." This document put forward ideas that were partly drawn from the American Declaration of Independence, published in 1776, to justify the rebellion against rule by Great Britain. It tells you a lot about the attitude of the old French government and aristocracy that saying that people had a right to their lives and their liberty was seen as a very dangerous statement!

In 1792 the people of Paris overthrew King Louis XVI. A National Convention was called to create a constitution and a government for France. Robespierre, with the backing of the Jacobins, was elected to head the Paris delegation to the Convention.

KING LOUIS XVI

Robespierre once argued strongly against the death penalty. But his positions shifted as the struggle between the revolutionary forces and those defending the old system continued. By December of 1793 he was arguing for the execution of the king—and won his argument.

THE RIGHTS OF MAN

There was a split in the revolution. On one side were people, like Robespierre, who believed strongly that all power should be shared out and that there should be no distinction between rich and poor, educated and unschooled. On the other side were people who wanted change, but did not see anything good coming from sharing out power with those who had no training or experience in running a government.

The main force on this side were the **Girondins**, and they were dominant in the first years of the revolution.

MONUMENT OF THE GIRONDINS

BANQUET OF THE GIRONDINS

The Girondins clearly saw the need for change, but they wanted improvements in the governance of France that would not do away with all of the traditions of France. For Robespierre and the Jacobins, that made the Girondins look very much like accomplices of the king and the nobility: the Girondins seemed to be trying to hang on to all the power and privileges they could for the wealthy and the powerful.

THE SANS-CULOTTES

Even further to the radical edge of politics than the Jacobins were the Sans-culottes ("without pants", referring to the traditional worker's clothing of a long smock held around the waist with a belt). The Sans-culottes were impatient for words to end and actions to start.

SANS-CULOTTES

They invaded, pillaged and burned country houses of rich landowners and nobles. They were not shy to kill those who resisted them. Robespierre increasingly adopted the phrases and fierceness of the Sans-culottes in his speeches.

In June, 1793, the Sans-culottes invaded the Convention and threw out the Girondins, whom they saw as committed to defending the monarchy and the rich. In their place, using threats of violence, they raised up the Jacobins.

THE ELIMINATION OF GIRONDINS

THE COMMITTEE OF PUBLIC SAFETY

At this point France was readying for war against several nations that were determined to overthrow the revolution and restore the monarchy, as well as royalist sympathizers within France. To manage the war effort, the Jacobins set up a "Committee for Public Safety". This body had broad powers over not just the army, but much of the government of France.

Robespierre became one of twelve members of the Committee in July, 1793. Until this point he had been an effective critic of the revolutionary government run by the Girondins. Now that he was in a position of power, he became intolerant of any disagreement.

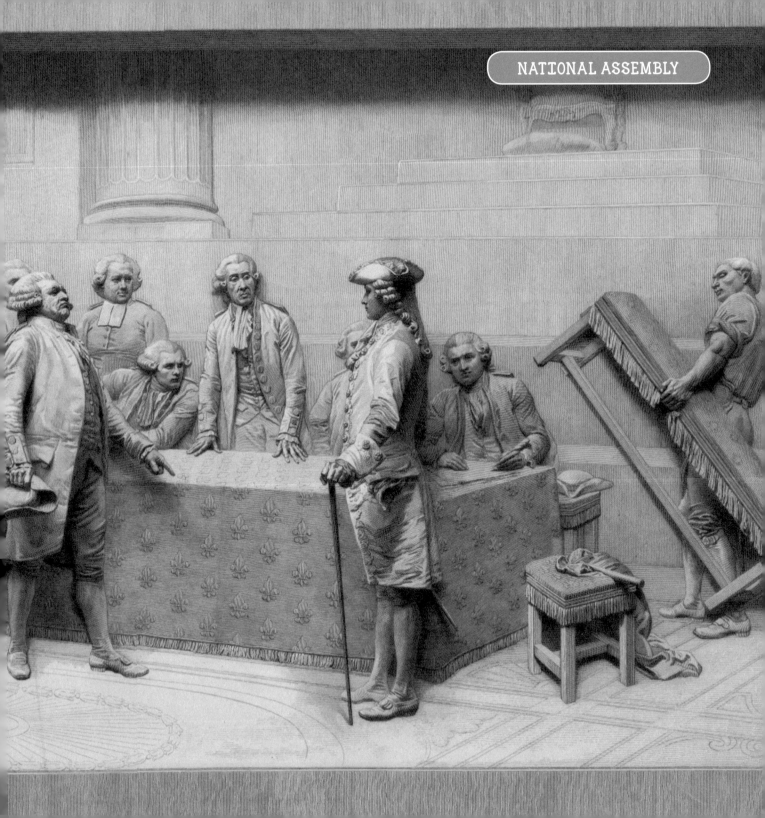

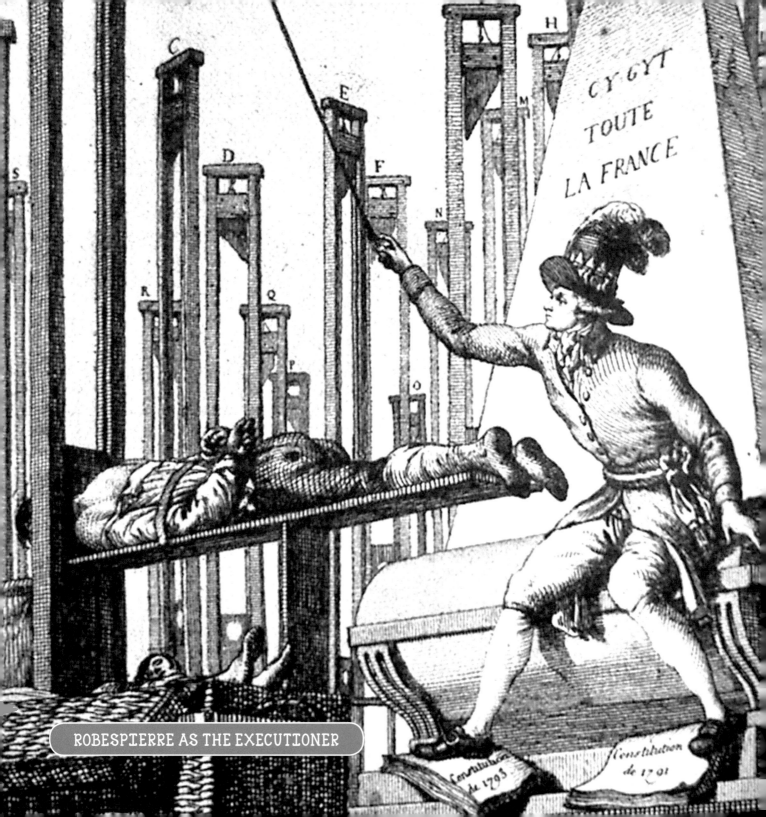

ROBESPIERRE AS THE EXECUTIONER

THE REIGN OF TERROR

Using defense of the revolution as its justification, the Committee brought in a program that came to be known as the "reign of terror" (read more about it in the Baby Professor book *Are You With Us or Against Us? Looking Back at the Reign of Terror*). Anyone suspected of opposing the revolution, or even disagreeing with the positions of the Jacobins, could be arrested or even executed. This was in response to increased pressure from the Sans-culottes to "make terror the theme of the day".

The new program suspended human rights and legal protections, and allowed government forces to use torture and imprisonment to shut down opposition. The Sans-culottes formed militias and took on some of the work of capturing or killing those they felt were not revolutionary enough.

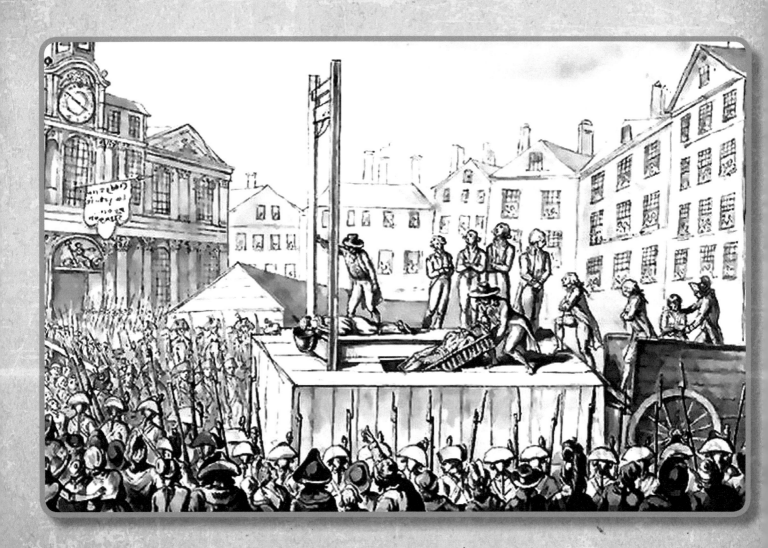

EXECUTION BY GUILLOTINE

The Reign of Terror began in September, 1793 and ran for about eleven months. During that time over 300,000 "enemies of the revolution" were arrested and over 17,000 were put to death. Robespierre used his power to make sure that many of his political opponents were among the victims. Many of the Girondin leaders were executed in this period along with members of the nobility, including Queen Marie Antoinette.

This was the first time in history that "terror" became the official policy of a government in power. Robespierre and others argued that terror now would make it possible to have a peaceful, harmonious world in the future.

EXECUTION KING LOUIS XVI

GOING TOO FAR

Robespierre was not the head of the Committee or the leader of the government. He was just one of twelve men directing the horrors of the Reign of Terror, but he was the most prominent. He also disagreed with many others on the Committee, who openly used the instruments of the Reign of Terror to enrich themselves and improve their position. Robespierre seemed to believe that the goal should be to use extreme measures to secure a more equal and more peaceful France, free of corruption.

Other members of the committee began to worry that Robespierre might soon turn his eye on their actions, and they decided to move first. In July, 1794, Robespierre and many of his supporters were arrested and executed.

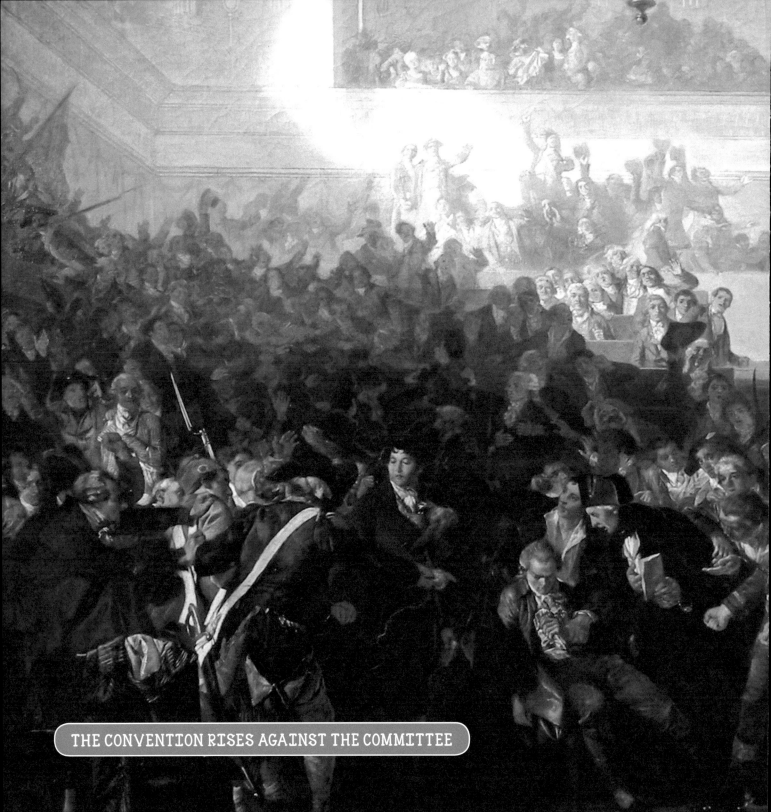

THE CONVENTION RISES AGAINST THE COMMITTEE

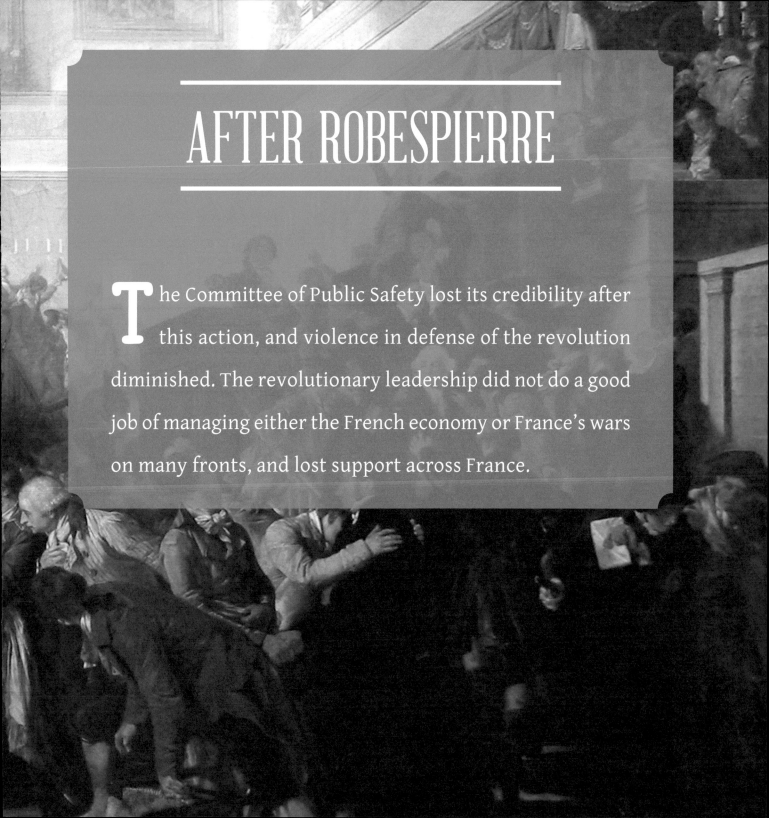

AFTER ROBESPIERRE

The Committee of Public Safety lost its credibility after this action, and violence in defense of the revolution diminished. The revolutionary leadership did not do a good job of managing either the French economy or France's wars on many fronts, and lost support across France.

Finally, in 1799, General Napoleon Bonaparte overthrew the revolutionary government and assumed the sole leadership of France. Later he declared himself its emperor.

NAPOLEON BONAPARTE

EXPLORE THE FRENCH REVOLUTION

The French Revolution was a turbulent time that affected more than just France. Learn more about the inspiring and terrible events of the Revolution in these Baby Professor books: *The French Revolution: People Power in Action*, *Moms Needed Bread: the Women's March on Versailles*, and *They Got Involved: The Famous People During the French Revolution*.

Visit

BABY PROFESSOR
EDUCATION KIDS

www.BabyProfessorBooks.com

to download Free Baby Professor eBooks
and view our catalog of new and exciting
Children's Books

Made in United States
Troutdale, OR
07/14/2023